What's for Dinner?

Quirky, Squirmy Poems
from the Animal World

Katherine B. Hauth

Illustrated by David Clark

Charlesbridge

This book is dedicated to Stephanie Farrow,
Lucy Hampson, Vaunda Micheaux Nelson,
Uma Krishnaswami, and Jeanne Whitehouse Peterson
for their inspiration and long-term encouragement
and insight.—K. B. H.

To my family—D. C.

Published by Charlesbridge
85 Main Street
Watertown, MA 02472
(617) 926-0329
www.charlesbridge.com

Library of Congress Cataloging-in-Publication Data
Hauth, Katherine B.
    What's for dinner?: quirky, squirmy poems from the animal world /
Katherine Hauth; illustrations by David Clark.
        p. cm.
    ISBN 978-1-57091-471-3 (reinforced for library use)
    ISBN 978-1-57091-472-0 (softcover)
    1. Predation (Biology)—Juvenile poetry. 2. Animals—Food—
Juvenile poetry. I. Clark, David, 1960 Mar. 19– ill. II. Title.
QL758.H378 2010
591.5'3—dc22   2010007588

Printed in China
(hc) 10 9 8 7 6 5 4 3 2 1
(sc) 10 9 8 7 6 5 4 3 2 1

Illustrations done in ink and watercolor on Arches paper
Display type set in P22 Mayflower and text type set in Adobe Caslon
Color separations by Chroma Graphics, Singapore
Printed and bound September 2010 by Jade Productions in Heyuan,
    Guangdong, China
Production supervision by Brian G. Walker
Designed by Susan Mallory Sherman

Table of Contents

What's for Dinner?

They might seek meat,
or nectar sweet,
the white of eggs,
or yolk,
sleek fish, dead trees,
fresh blood, live bees,
or prickly artichoke.

But finding food
is not a joke.
Living things must eat
or croak.

Food Chain

Painted lady butterfly   whiptail lizard   garter snake
        now reside   one inside   the other

                all inside
                roadrunner.

Fast Food

Scree! Scree!
Male hawk calls
opens claws
    lets

        snake

           f

         a

        l

      l

        Female
    flying below
   flips back
       jackknifes
  talons snatch
         the twisting
      snake

     Scree!

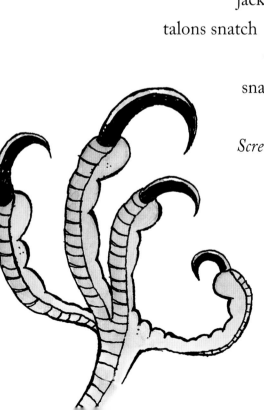

Waste Management

No dainty vegetarian,
the vulture rips up carrion.
It likes to feast before the worms,
which saves us all from stink and germs.

In the Pink

In a stilt-walk
water dance,
flamingos
sift for food,
heads upside down,
under water,
in the middle
of the muddle
of the mud.

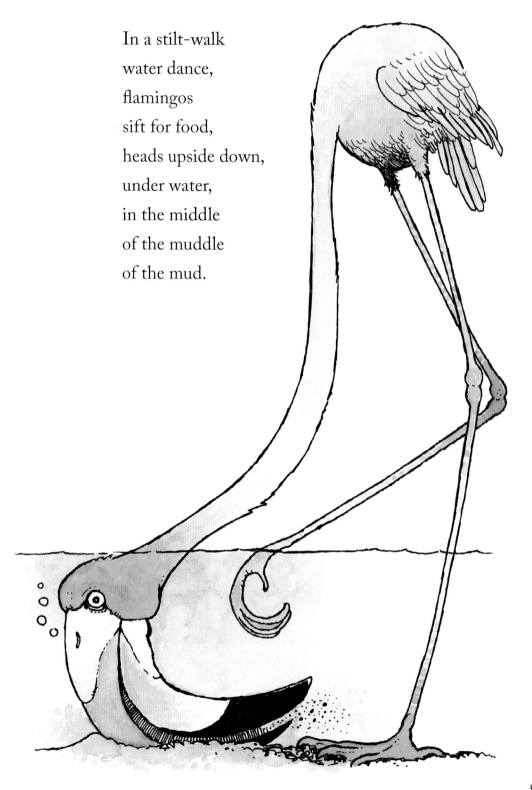

Nighthawk

Insect catcher,

how do you swallow
each night
in full flight
three thousand
resisting
fast-kicking
throat-tickling
legs
?

Late Late Show

Flying at night
Little brown bat
Strikes insects with its wings
Forms a bowl by curving its tail
Scoops up the stunned
And eats them
          Mostly
     one   by   one
          like
     p o p c o r n.

Spinning for Supper

(One Water Bird's Way)

The phalarope
      spins
'round in a tizzy
      spins
without getting dizzy
      spins
sixty turns a minute
raising a water
tornado
with dinner in it.

Mayflies,

wing-dancing over water,
did you
       mate
  and
        lay your eggs
    before
       the swallow came?

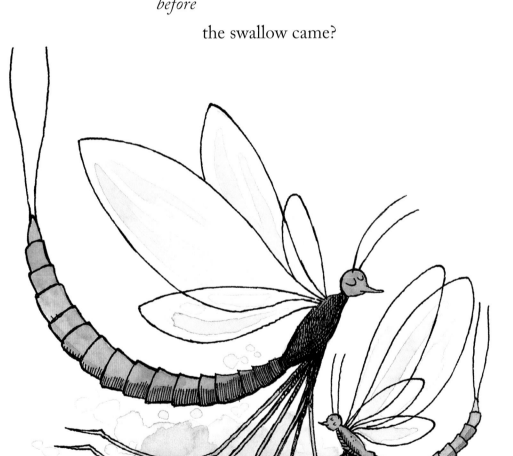

Sharp Shooter

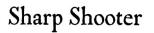

Archer Fish:
snout like a gun,
gills as trigger,
blasts insects
with bullets of water

                    leaps
Then
to catch
its falling prey.

A *grand jeté*
    in a life-and-death ballet.

Blink of an Eye

Butterfly flits by

hungry mouth of leaping trout

quick raccoon hooks lunch.

Wood Turtle Stomp

Stompin' its feet
and slammin' its shell
to the ancient beat
it knows so well.

Stompin' an' slammin'
Stompin' an' slammin'
'til worms pop up
to see who's jammin'.

Slammin' an' stompin'
Slammin' an' stompin'.
Soon wood turtle's chompin'
on squirmy sweet meat.

Four Ways to Catch a Seal

Alone in her cold Arctic home
Polar Bear hunts.

1.

Catching a scent from a distant ice floe
She submarines toward it—unseen below.

     Snags her seal with a single blow.

2.

Like a mound of snow,
By a seal's breathing hole Polar Bear waits.

     Seal pops up for air. Sees bear.   Too late!

3.

Smelling a meal on the vast, treeless snow
She flattens her body and s-l-o-w-l-y creeps.

     Catches the seal asleep.

4.

Sniffing the snow, she discovers seal's den,
Then jumps up and down till the roof caves in.

     Traps her prey within.

Through whiteout and wind and subzero chill
Polar Bear hunts.

Marabou Storks

It's not the hunt makes these storks thrill;
their forte lies in standing still.

While hyenas snarl at vultures,
they hang back like ugly sculptures.

They wait.

(When others' appetites are filled,
there's much less risk of getting killed.)

Night Notes

Hyena looks quite musical
　　　hauling xylophone around.

But this here's no gig—
　　　them's someone's ribs!

Age-Old Alliance

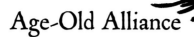

Throughout the year, ravens follow
howls of hunting wolves.
Following howls, following wolves,
leads hungry ravens to food.
    After wolves have eaten their fill
    enough is left for ravens' meal.

But winter's cold and long.
Snow falls fast and deep.
Wolves hunker in snow.
Ravens huddle in trees.
    Days go by.
    No food to eat.

When at last the storm abates
travel for wolves is hard and slow
through the deeply drifted snow.
Ravens lift on swift wing beats
    scouting forests, scanning hills
    trying to spot a winter kill.

Keen eyes spy a carcass!

But they still can starve—for raven beaks,
designed for tearing meat from bone,
find hide of elk is tough,
their beaks not strong enough.
        Ravens shout loud, raspy calls.
        Wolves start toward the meal.

Escort ravens guide the wolves
who bring the needed tools—
strong jaws, sharp teeth—
to carve the frozen feast.

        Wolves *and* ravens eat.

Inside and Outside the Sloth

Sloth's brown, but looks green
so he blends in with his tree,
chomping its leaves,
while hundreds of beetles and moths
on Sloth's back, feed on the algae
that turn his hair green.

In the gut of the Sloth, bacteria teem
feasting on pulverized leaves,
breaking them down for Sloth to digest—
using some nutrients, passing the rest.

On the weekly occasion of Sloth's defecation
he ever-so-slowly
    climbs
        down
            to
                the
                    ground
to poop and pee beneath his tree.

Insects living on Sloth
quickly jump off
to lay their eggs on his dung—
with its sugar and starch
that will nourish their young.

What insects don't eat
will feed the Sloth's tree.

Beetles and moths of several species,
which laid their eggs on the feces,
jump back onto the back of the Sloth
for the l o n g s l o w ride
to the tree's canopy
for another week.

And then repeat.

Sloth in a tree, bacteria, leaves,
beetles, moths, and algae,
insect young on Sloth's fresh dung:

Quite a menagerie,
feeding in harmony.

The Nose Knows

The scent
of fallen fig seeds
calls a rat to feed.

Rat's aroma
brings a boa
to its furry prey.

Rat gets a hug today.

On the Wing

Holding its legs
like a basket
of stickers and spines,

Dragonfly
catches insects,
quickly dines

on the wing

shimmering.

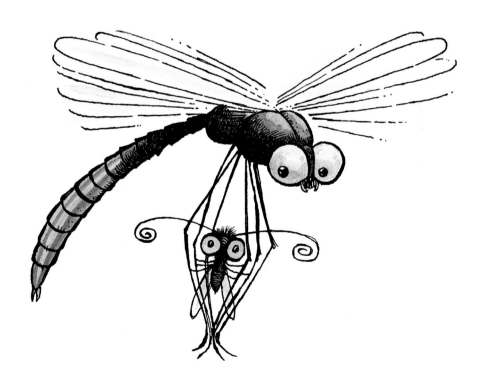

Mosquitoes,

with needle-noses
sucking blood
from elbows, cheeks, and chin,

why were you not
designed to thrive
on brine, on swine,
or likewise-spiny
porcupines?

SLAP!

SLAP!

SLAP!

Cowgirl Spider

She lures a distant moth with sweet-deceit perfume.
He flies swiftly toward her, thinking *honeymoon*.

Skilled Bolas Spider twirls silk lasso in night air,
Rounds up the moth she's tricked to her sticky snare.

Fancy twirler,
        tricky spinner,
spider cowgirl
        catches dinner.

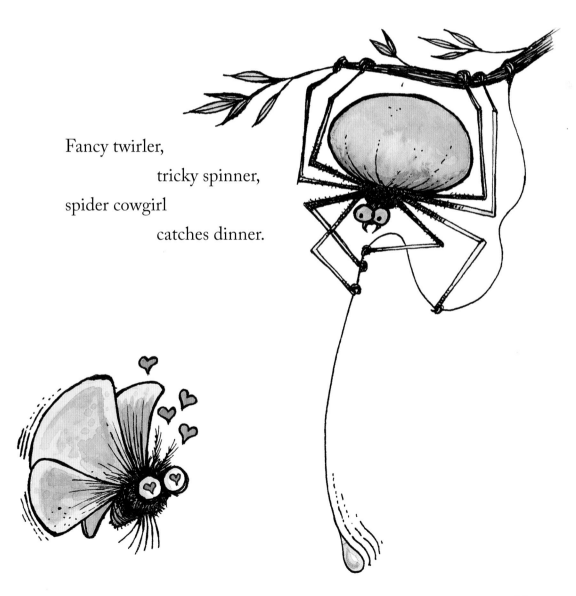

Dermestid Beetles Wanted

Unique opportunity!

Create eyeless sculptures for display.

Work quick, work neat,

leave no scratch, no nick.

Gnaw soft flesh from skulls.

Clear throats, polish teeth,

pick brains and nostrils clean.

Apply: Chicago Field Museum.

Preying Praying Mantis

She turns around,
Gives him a peck,
Severs his head
Right off his neck.

Poor Mr. Mantis,
His merciless Missus
Devours her mate.

He tastes delicious!

Neat Feet

Butterfly
tippy-toes on marigold,
daisy, peony, and rose,
finding what is good to eat,
tasting flowers with its feet.

Road-Toad Restaurant

In adjoining banquet rooms, they dine *al fresco*—
upper thigh for ants, lower thigh for wasps.
They feast till full.

Beneath a canopy of mottled skin—
above the flattened torso—
flies make reservations for their young.

Bad Landing

If horsefly sets
on Venus flytrap,
you can bet—
that horsefly
will get et.

Baby Wasps

They hatch in the dark
    all wiggly and squirmy
        where they eat what is there
all lunching and munching
    increasing their girth
till they burst
    (still wriggly and wormy)
        from the skin
of the fine caterpillar
    their mom had selected
        for dinner.

Not a Banana

With the color of banana
the shape of banana
the size of banana
this not-a-banana
needs no shell
to hide inside
as it slowly glides
slowly rides.

Mole spies it, expects
to banana-slug dine.

Mole easily grabs it.
      Gags   and ejects it!

Slug glides away on its mouth-numbing slime.

Eating Words

When you know
that *vore* means *eat,*
you will know
that **insectivores** feed
>   on grasshoppers, moths, and butterflies,
>   mosquitoes, bees, and plain-old flies.

When you know
that *carni* means *meat,*
you will know
that **carnivores** eat
>   snakes and lizards, deer and lamb,
>   carrion, birds, fish, and ham.

When you know
that *herb* means *plant,*
you will know
that **herbivores** CAN'T
>   eat anything that moves on foot,
>   just foods that spring up from a root.

When you know
that *omni* means *all*,
you will know
that **omnivores** call

Everything
 they can suck or chew—
 sometimes even me or you—
food.

More Words About the Poems

Scientific words help to tell more exactly what's happening as creatures eat. Many of these poems are about *predators* that hunt other animals. Their victims are called *prey.* "Food Chain" shows how predators can become prey for bigger, faster, stronger predators. Even though humans are at the top of the *food chain,* "Mosquitoes" shows that humans can be prey too. *Prey* is also a verb. In "Preying Praying Mantis" the female mantis preys upon her mate. Most animals don't eat their own kind, or *species.* Those that do are called *cannibals.* This cannibal mating habit guarantees the female mantis will have nourishment to produce healthy young.

Scavengers eat nature's leftovers. In "Marabou Storks" the birds will feed on dead meat, or *carrion,* killed by another animal. (A single dead body is also called a *carcass.*) Some scavengers feed on rotting leaves, fruit, or even dung, like the moth's young in "Inside and Outside the Sloth."

Much of the world's dining is done on dung. Think of it. Everything that eats and drinks needs to excrete leftover waste. If animals didn't recycle that excrement, we might be walking waist-high in it. Recycling is the natural way of things.

Symbiosis refers to the relationships among different species that live closely together. When symbiosis benefits both ravens and wolves, as in "Age-Old Alliance," it's called *mutualism.* In "Baby Wasps" the relationship between the wasps and the caterpillar is called *parasitism.* It benefits the wasps but kills the caterpillar. The wasps are *parasites,* meaning they harm or kill the *host* they live on.

"Inside and Outside the Sloth" shows many creatures eating together without competition or injury to the others. This type of symbiosis is known as *commensalism.* The sloth is neither helped nor harmed by the insects that live on it.

Every food chain in these poems links to other food chains. Each one is part of the greater *web of life.* We don't understand how all of the pieces fit together in nature's great puzzle, but we come closer to seeing the whole picture as we learn more about relationships between plants, between animals, and between plants and animals.

Scientifically or poetically, nature reveals unlimited, amazing variety.

More Words About the Animals

"What's for Dinner?"

Whether they dine on bees, trees, or artichokes, every creature eats. Colorful birds called bee-eaters catch bees in flight, then land and swallow them—after first removing the stinger. Colonies of termites thrive on wood. Many insects, as well as slugs and snails, enjoy snacking on artichokes, much to the dismay of human gardeners. Whatever the diet, the eater is eaten—sooner or later—by something else.

"Food Chain"

Roadrunners eat almost everything: insects, fruit, small animals, and eggs. During spring courtship, the male often wins his mate by offering her a lizard. Because road-runners are so fast and their beaks so sharp, they can kill rattlesnakes! Then they slowly swallow them headfirst.

"Fast Food"

Hawk experts think that the acrobatic feat of two hawks playing catch with a free-falling snake—an unusual sighting—is part of their courtship ritual. The *scree* call identifies the pair as red-tailed hawks, which mate for the life of the pair.

"Waste Management"

Turkey vultures don't have strong beaks and feet. They can't tear into tough hide and muscle until it's been "tenderized" by decay. A turkey vulture's featherless red head and neck may look strange, but skin is easier to clean than feathers after the bird plunges its head into a rotting carcass.

"In the Pink"

A flamingo's beak and feet stir up microscopic animals, algae, small crustaceans, fish, and mollusks for the bird to eat. The food contains carotenes—pigments or coloring material—that turn the flamingo's otherwise white feathers pink. (Carrots that we eat contain carotenes too, but we don't eat enough carrots to turn color.)

"Nighthawk"

The common nighthawk is not a hawk and doesn't tend to fly at night. It usually hunts in the evening, on the edge of night. This North American bird's other name, "goatsucker," originated long ago. When goatherds saw the nighthawk's European relatives flying open-mouthed near their herds, they thought the birds drank milk from the goats' teats.

"Late Late Show"

Bat diets range from fruit, pollen, and nectar to fish and blood, but 70 percent of bats eat insects. Bats locate their prey by sending out high-frequency sounds that echo off objects in their path. This technique is called echolocation.

"Spinning for Supper"

Phalaropes spin in deep water to find food such as insect larvae, tiny shrimp, and fish. When scientists timed the red-necked phalarope in a laboratory experiment, they found that the bird could spin as fast as sixty times a minute. The spinning creates a central vacuum that sucks up water, along with prey.

"Mayflies"

Some people call mayflies "day flies" because the entire adult life of most species takes place within a day—sometimes within a few hours. The adult stage is spent mating and laying eggs. Adult mayflies don't eat, but they are welcome food for birds and fish.

"Sharp Shooter"

This poem combines two hunting techniques of the archer fish, which can leap to catch low-flying prey and can shoot powerful jets of water to knock more distant prey into the water. This Asian and Australian fish can shoot accurately to more than 6 feet (1.8 meters).

"Blink of an Eye"

Raccoons usually live near water and eat a wide variety of plants and animals. Long toes on their front paws are as nimble as fingers but have sharp claws—just right for grasping a slippery fish.

"Wood Turtle Stomp"

Wood turtles live primarily in the northeastern and north-central United States near water in open woodlands. Scientists think the vibrations caused by their stomping may sound like rain to worms below. The worms respond by wriggling to the surface. Oops! Wrong move—for the worms.

"Four Ways to Catch a Seal"

The polar bear is a well-equipped hunter with strong, massive paws, good eyesight, and a keen sense of smell. The bear's favorite food is seal, which supplies the bear with fat to survive cold Arctic weather. During the summer the bear may also eat birds, eggs, mushrooms, and berries, as well as seaweed.

"Marabou Storks"

These African storks often play a waiting game to scavenge at carcasses. They also hunt at rubbish dumps and at drying pools, where they can pick off stranded water creatures. Attracted to grass fires from long distances, marabou storks patrol the fire's edge to catch fleeing animals.

"Night Notes"

Spotted hyenas are the largest and most common hyena in Africa. Hunting in female-led clans, they kill up to 90 percent of their food. They also loot the kills of others. One spotted hyena can quickly gorge up to 33 pounds (15 kilograms) of meat, which it eats bones and all. Brown and striped hyenas are mostly scavengers.

"Age-Old Alliance"

Ravens follow the howls and trails of wolves for most of the year. In winter ravens have been observed calling loudly upon finding a frozen carcass. Possibly drawn by the ravens' calls, wolves soon arrive and tear open the tough hide of the fallen animal.

"Inside and Outside the Sloth"

In the sloth's dense hair, its hitchhikers aren't easy to see. Researchers had to get up close to discover nine species of moth, four species of beetle, six species of tick, and three species of algae on a single sloth. Another researcher counted up to one hundred moths on one sloth. Sloths live in Central and South American rain forests.

"The Nose Knows"

Boa constrictors wrap themselves tightly around their prey. This squeezes or constricts the prey's lungs till it can't breathe and dies of suffocation. Boa constrictors are found primarily from northern Mexico to northern Argentina.

"On the Wing"

Dragonflies are well designed for hunting on the wing. Their four wings work separately so they can hover in the air or move straight up and down, backward, or sideways. This agile flyer's head can turn almost all the way around, and its huge eyes with thirty thousand lenses see in all directions. Hunting on the wing is called "hawking."

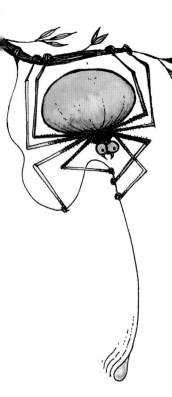

"Mosquitoes"

What looks like a "needle-nose" on a mosquito is its proboscis. This hollow tube allows mosquitoes to suck liquids. Male and female mosquitoes feed on flower nectar and plant juices. Only the female needs to suck blood to develop eggs.

"Cowgirl Spider"

At night, at the edge of its web, the bolas spider twirls a line of silk like a lasso. A sticky blob at the end smells like a female moth. When a male moth flies near, the spider tries to snag it with the blob. (Cowboys in Argentina swing a leather cord with two or three heavy balls, called a *bola*. The twirling balls tangle around a calf's legs and bring it down. The bolas spider is named after this technique.)

"Dermestid Beetles Wanted"

Dermestid beetles are the same small beetles you see "disposing of" dead animals on the road. Museums often keep a colony of these beetles to clean bones for their exhibits. The larvae, which eat the fastest, do most of the work. Between "meaty" projects, the colony can eat dry cat food.

"Preying Praying Mantis"

The praying mantis waits in a prayer-like pose for prey to come within range of its lightning-quick, powerful front legs. Mantises eat mostly insects, including their own kind. Large species found in the tropics can also catch hummingbirds, frogs, and snakes.

"Neat Feet"

A butterfly has no mouth. It tastes with its feet. When it finds a nutritious flower, it straightens its curled proboscis like a straw to sip the flower's nectar. Before laying her eggs, the female butterfly tastes leaves to select those that her young can eat.

"Road-Toad Restaurant"
Different insects like dinner at different stages of decay, so they tend to feed on separate parts of the same carcass. Wasps and ants may strip meat to feed their larvae. Adult flies prefer gooey food, but they lay their eggs ("make reservations for their young") on solid meat that their larvae will eat.

"Bad Landing"
When an insect brushes against the trigger hairs of a Venus flytrap, the hinged leaf snaps shut in one-tenth of a second—even faster in full sunlight. These plants, which live in low-nutrient soil, benefit from an occasional high-protein, insect "power snack."

"Baby Wasps"
The female braconid wasp in this poem laid her eggs inside a tomato hornworm caterpillar. Inside the caterpillar, the wasp larvae hatch and eat their way to maturity. They eat fat and muscle first, saving the heart and central nervous system till the end. When the larvae mature, they crawl out and weave cocoons on the caterpillar's skin. The caterpillar may not die until after the adult wasps emerge a few days later from their cocoons.

"Not a Banana"
Unlike their snail relatives, slugs have no protective shell. The Pacific Coast banana slug substitutes mouth-numbing slime to discourage predators. This North American slug usually grows to about 6 inches (15 centimeters) long, but some have been known to reach 10 inches (25 centimeters). They scavenge on fallen fruit and leaves, as well as animal feces and carrion.

Where to Learn More About the Animals in This Book

Animal Sharpshooters by Anthony D. Fredericks (Franklin Watts, 1999)

Are You a Dragonfly? by Judy Allen (Kingfisher, 2001)

Baby Sloth by Aubrey Lang (Fitzhenry & Whiteside, 2004)

Bats by Adrienne Mason (Kids Can Press, 1992)

Bats by Gail Gibbons (Holiday House, 1999)

Creepy Crawly Baby Bugs by Sandra Markle (Walker and Company, 1996)

Dragonflies by Patrick Merrick (The Child's World, 2007)

Encyclopedia of Extremely Weird Animals by Sarah Lovett (John Muir, 1997)

Extremely Weird Bats by Sarah Lovett (John Muir, 1992)

Mud City, A Flamingo Story by Brenda Z. Guiberson (Henry Holt, 2005)

Paisano, the Roadrunner by Jennifer Owings Dewey (Millbrook Press, 2002)

Polar Bear: Animals in Danger by Rod Theodorou (Heinemann First Library, 2001)

Polar Bears by Lesley A. DuTemple (Lerner Early Bird Nature Book, 1997)

Sloths by Melissa Stewart (Carolrhoda, 2005)

Wild Flamingos by Bruce McMillan (Houghton Mifflin, 1997)

The Wolf: Night Howler (Animal Close-Ups series) by Christian Havard (Charlesbridge, 2006)